A Gift For _Kayson Martin_

From _Nana + Pappy Grove_

How to Use Your Interactive Storybook & Story Buddy™:

1. Activate your Story Buddy™ by pressing the "On / Off" button on the ear.
2. Read the story aloud in a quiet place. Speak in a clear voice when you see the highlighted phrases.
3. Listen to your Story Buddy™ respond with several different phrases throughout the book.

Clarity and speed of reading affect the way Christopher™ responds. He may not always respond to young children.

Watch for even more interactive Storybooks & Story Buddy™ characters. For more information, visit us on the Web at www.Hallmark.com/StoryBuddy.

Copyright © 2011 Hallmark Licensing, Inc.

Published by Hallmark Gift Books,
a division of Hallmark Cards, Inc.,
Kansas City, MO 64141
Visit us on the Web at www.Hallmark.com.

Editor: Emily Osborn
Art Director: Kevin Swanson
Designer: Mary Eakin
Production Artist: Dan Horton

ISBN: 978-1-59530-459-9
KOB8046
Printed and bound in China
SEP11

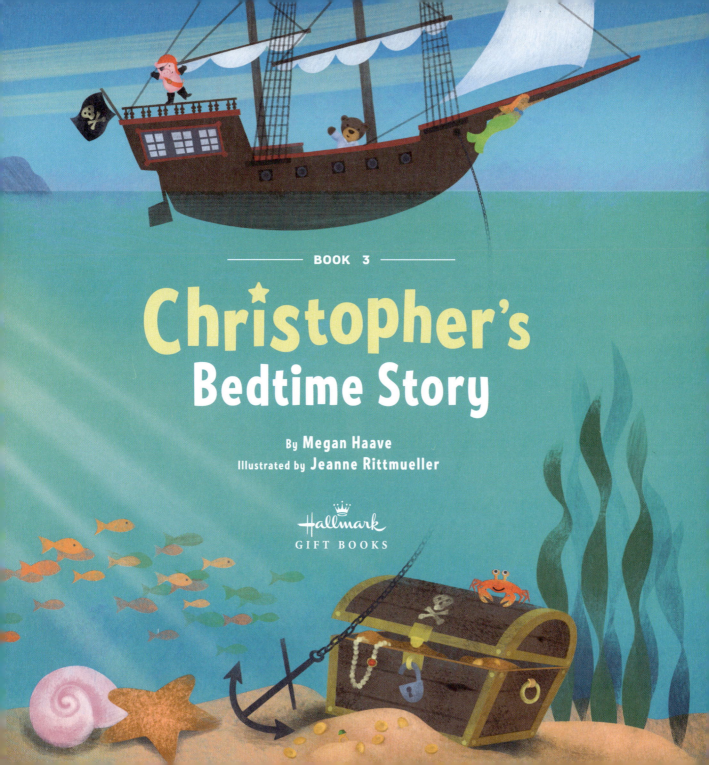

BOOK 3

Christopher's
Bedtime Story

By **Megan Haave**
Illustrated by **Jeanne Rittmueller**

Hallmark
GIFT BOOKS

Christopher had a full day. He brushed his teeth. He put on his pajamas. And now it was time for a bedtime story.

Christopher got in bed and listened closely as Dad read *Dinosaurs in Space*. When they were done, Dad closed the book and said, "Now it's time to say good night."

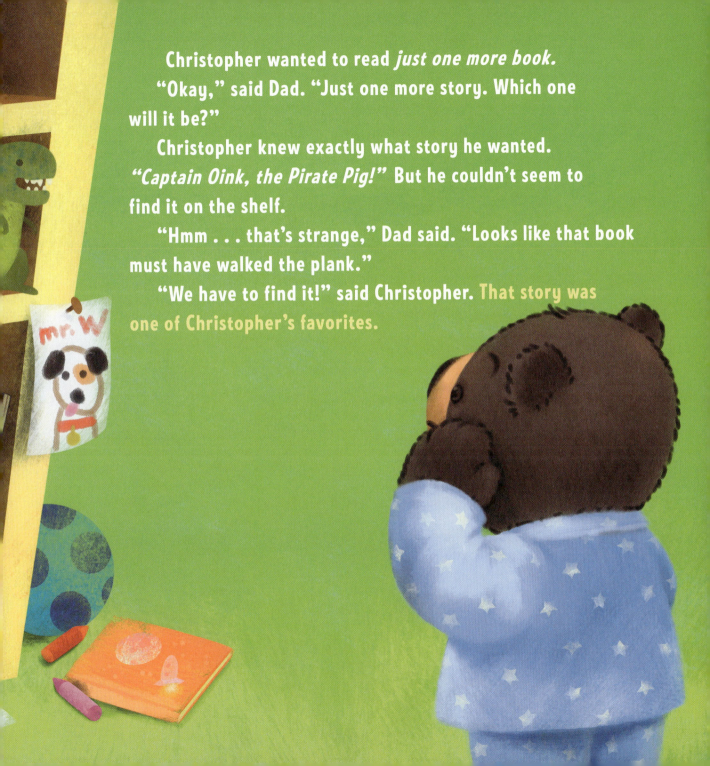

Christopher wanted to read *just one more book.*

"Okay," said Dad. "Just one more story. Which one will it be?"

Christopher knew exactly what story he wanted. *"Captain Oink, the Pirate Pig!"* But he couldn't seem to find it on the shelf.

"Hmm . . . that's strange," Dad said. "Looks like that book must have walked the plank."

"We have to find it!" said Christopher. That story was one of Christopher's favorites.

Christopher had no idea where the book could be. "Where should I look?" he asked Dad.

"Hmm, let's think. Remember when Captain Oink was looking for his lost treasure?" Dad asked. "What was the first thing he did?"

"The first thing . . . the first thing . . ." Christopher thought long and hard.

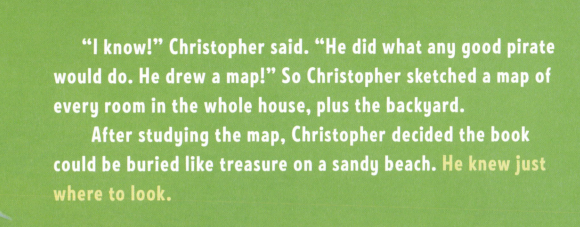

"I know!" Christopher said. "He did what any good pirate would do. He drew a map!" So Christopher sketched a map of every room in the whole house, plus the backyard.

After studying the map, Christopher decided the book could be buried like treasure on a sandy beach. He knew just where to look.

Christopher and Dad raced to the backyard. He dug through every inch of the sandbox, but the only thing he uncovered was a toy car he'd lost the week before. No book.

Christopher frowned. "It wasn't where I thought it would be. What do I do now?"

Dad reminded him, "You know when Captain Oink tried to think of the safest place his treasure could be?" Christopher thought long and hard.

"The safest place?" Christopher wondered. All this thinking was making him sleepy. "Well, the safest place for his treasure was beside the Snorting Sea Beast, who guarded it from thieves." Just then, Christopher heard a sound from the kitchen. A snorting sound. He knew just where to look.

Christopher tiptoed into the kitchen. The sound was
coming from his dog, Mr. Waffles. But this beast wasn't
snorting. He was *snoring*. Mr. Waffles was always
dragging Christopher's things back to his "lair." The
book had to be around here somewhere.

Christopher looked around, on top, even *under* the big snoring dog. Mr. Waffles definitely did not have his book. Christopher wondered if he snored when he was asleep.
"So much for guarding my treasure," he thought. Watching Mr. Waffles sleep, Christopher was getting pretty tired.

"What do I do now?" Christopher asked Dad. "I've looked in all the places I thought it could be and—" he rubbed his eyes, "I'm running out of time."

Dad thought for a minute. "Maybe you need to look at things from a new angle. You know, like when Captain Oink needed to see the *whole* island instead of just a piece of it."

Christopher thought long and hard.

Christopher remembered that Captain Oink didn't have time to walk around the whole island. He needed to find his treasure fast. Then Christopher remembered that the Captain got a better view by climbing up into the crow's nest of his ship. From there, he could see the entire island all at once.

"Shiver me timbers!" Christopher said. He knew just where to look.

Christopher went back to his room and climbed right up the ladder of his bunk bed. And there it was, right where Christopher had left it the night before. He felt proud of his treasure-hunting success, but also Christopher was feeling really sleepy.

Christopher smiled and handed the book to Dad. "I found my treasure, Matey!" "And just before bedtime," said Dad. "You are quite the pirate . . . quite the sleepy pirate." After all that searching, Christopher was ready for bed.

As happy as Christopher had been to find his favorite book, he was even happier to have Dad read it to him. When they were finished, Dad gave Christopher a good night kiss. He closed the book and put it back on the shelf where it belonged. Then he turned off the light.

"Sweet dreams, Christopher."

Did you have fun reading with Christopher™?
We would love to hear from you!

Please send your comments to:
Hallmark Book Feedback
P.O. Box 419034
Mail Drop 215
Kansas City, MO 64141

Or e-mail us at:
booknotes@hallmark.com